Princess Frederica CE Primary School

This book was presented to Princess
Frederica by :

Maureen Speller

Date: May 2002

WILD·WORLD·OF·ANIMALS

GRASSLANDS & PRAIRIES

MICHAEL CHINERY
ILLUSTRATED BY JOHN BUTLER
AND BRIAN MCINTYRE

Kingfisher Books

Kingfisher Books, Grisewood & Dempsey Ltd,
Elsley House, 24–30 Great Titchfield Street,
London W1P 7AD

First published in 1991 by Kingfisher Books

BRITISH LIBRARY CATALOGUING IN PUBLICATION DATA
Chinery, Michael *1938–*
    Grasslands and Prairies.
    1. Grasslands. Animals
    I. Title II. Butler, John *1952–* III. McIntyre, Brian
    IV. Series
    591.90953
ISBN 0 86272 726 X

Series editor: Mike Halson
Series designer: Terry Woodley
Designer: Dave West Children's Books
Illustrators: John Butler (pp. 1, 4–11, 16–17, 20–21,
26–27, 32–37); Brian McIntyre (pp. 2–3, 12–15, 18–19,
22–25, 28–31, 38)
Cover illustrations: John Butler

Phototypeset by Southern Positives and Negatives
(SPAN), Lingfield, Surrey. Printed and bound in
Hong Kong.

Contents

Life in the grasslands

The picture below shows the African savanna, or grassland. The main plants here are grasses. Natural grasslands like this are found in places with regular rainfall, but not enough rain for many trees to grow. The rain falls only at one time of the year and makes the grass grow quickly. Herds of antelope and other grazing animals move over the grasslands looking for this fresh grass. Lions and other meat-eaters follow them as they go.

GRASSLAND FACTS

● Grasslands of some kind or other make up over one quarter of the world's vegetation.

● Grasslands stretch almost unbroken from Hungary to China – a distance of more than 6000 km.

DO YOU KNOW

Not all of the world's grasslands are natural. The grassy fields and hillsides of Europe were once covered with trees, but people cut them down to make way for sheep and cattle. Through their grazing, these animals stop trees from growing again.

NATURAL GRASSLANDS

This map shows the world's main natural grasslands. Those in North America are called prairies, while those in Africa are called savannas. The cool grasslands of Asia and eastern Europe are known as steppes. South America's cool grasslands are called the pampas, while the warmer ones, nearer the Equator, are known as the campos.

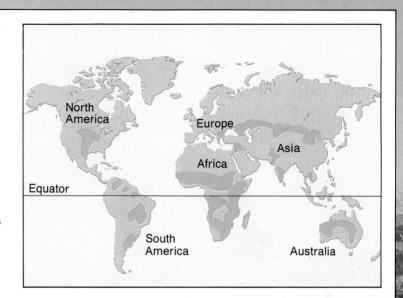

DO YOU KNOW

All grassland animals depend on the grass. Some animals eat the grass itself, while others feed on these grass-eaters.

During each month of the rainy season, 1 square kilometre of African grassland produces over 500 tonnes of grass. This is enough food to feed about 30 small antelope.

Elephants – giants of the grasslands

African elephants are the world's largest land animals. They have the biggest ears and the longest noses. They also have the biggest appetites. A male can weigh as much as eight family cars and needs over 200 kg of food every day. It feeds for up to 16 hours a day – mainly on grass. Elephants also push trees down to eat the leaves and fruit, and they rip off the bark with their tusks to get at the juicy layers underneath.

DO YOU KNOW

Thirsty elephants dig for water with their tusks. Male elephants also fight with their big tusks.

Male elephants are called bulls, females are called cows, and babies are called calves. The calves are very hairy when they are born and they can walk when they are only one hour old!

ELEPHANT FACTS

- An elephant's ivory tusks are sometimes 3 metres long.

- Elephants can sleep standing up, but they never sleep for long.

- African elephants can live for about 70 years.

Elephants greet their friends by shaking trunks, just as we shake hands. They live in large family groups called herds.

An elephant's trunk is a combined nose and upper lip. It is used to breathe, smell, feed and drink, and even to make noises.

Elephants use their trunks to squirt dust and water all over themselves. The dust helps to protect them from sunburn.

SURVIVAL WATCH

Adult elephants have no natural enemies, but people kill them for their ivory tusks and their numbers have been greatly reduced. Trade in ivory has now been banned, so hopefully the elephants will be left to roam the grasslands in peace.

The elephant's huge ears help it to keep cool by giving off heat. The hotter it is, the harder the elephant flaps its ears.

Ostriches – the world's biggest birds

The ostrich is a bird, but it can't fly. Its wings are much too small to carry its large body. A male ostrich can be 2.5 metres high and weigh over 130 kg. It can run across the African grassland at speeds of over 60 km/h. Ostriches eat almost anything they can find. In some parts of Africa the birds are reared on farms for their skins and meat.

? DO YOU KNOW

The male ostrich usually has several wives and they all lay their eggs in the same nest. There may be 30 eggs in the nest. Each egg can weigh up to 1 kg. They hatch after about six weeks.

Ostrich feathers are large and fluffy and were once widely used to decorate ladies' clothes and hats.

The ostrich has only two large toes on each foot. The toes are very tough and are used for defence.

The ostrich's tough skin can be turned into good-quality leather for making shoes and handbags.

The long-necked giraffe

The giraffe grows up to 5.5 metres tall. It lives on the African savanna, where its long legs and long neck enable it to reach the leaves of the prickly acacia trees. Giraffes defend themselves with their hooves and a single kick can kill a lion. Few animals will attack them, but hunters have killed all the giraffes in some parts of Africa.

The giraffe's long tongue rips leaves and twigs from the acacia's branches. The thorns don't seem to hurt it.

Giraffes walk slowly, moving the two legs on one side together, while balancing on the other two.

Giraffes use their short, skin-covered horns to keep the spiny branches away from their eyes.

DO YOU KNOW

The giraffe has to do the splits in order to drink. Its blood vessels are specially designed to prevent too much blood from gushing to its head while it is drinking.

The giraffe's neck has the same number of bones as yours – just seven. But of course they are much longer in the giraffe.

The speedy cheetah

The cheetah is the fastest animal on four legs. Two seconds after starting, it can be running at 72 km/h. Long legs give this big cat the speed it needs to catch antelope on the African savanna. It can cover several metres in a single bound. Cheetahs live in small groups and the mother teaches her cubs how to hunt. They hunt during the day, usually early in the morning and late in the afternoon when it is not too hot.

If a cheetah doesn't catch its prey within about 400 metres, it gives up and looks for another animal to chase. This cheetah has just missed the gazelle it was chasing.

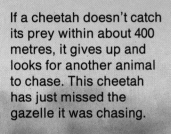

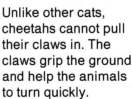

Unlike other cats, cheetahs cannot pull their claws in. The claws grip the ground and help the animals to turn quickly.

 CHEETAH FACTS

- The cheetah looks like a leopard, but you can identify it by the black stripes on its face.

- The cheetah is about 2 metres long from its nose to the tip of its tail.

- It can reach speeds up to 100 km/h, but only for a few seconds at a time.

Swarming locusts

Locusts are big grasshoppers which live in dry grasslands. When heavy rain makes the grass grow well in one area, lots of locusts gather there to feed. They all lay their eggs there and the baby locusts stay together when they hatch. Something keeps them together even when they grow up, and they fly off in a huge swarm. They destroy crops and other plants wherever they land. A really big locust swarm is called a plague.

There are several kinds of locusts. The kind pictured here is the desert locust of Africa, Arabia, and India.

 DO YOU KNOW

Baby locusts are called hoppers. They march over the ground and eat the plants as they go. They have no wings at first. They change their skins five times as they grow up and their wings appear on their backs.

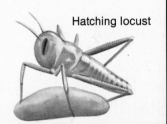

Hatching locust

A locust swarm may contain as many as a billion insects, together weighing 1,500,000 kg. It can completely blacken the sky.

LOCUST FACTS

● The desert locust is about 7 cm long. It weighs about 1.5 gm.

● A swarm of desert locusts can travel over 200 km in a day, eating 1,500,000 kg of food on the way. The complete trail of damage may stretch for over 3000 km.

The locust chews leaves with its strong jaws. Each insect eats its own weight of food every day.

The short-sighted rhinoceros

Next to the elephant, the rhinoceros is the world's biggest land animal. Africa's white rhinoceros, which isn't really white, weighs up to 5 tonnes. It is a peaceful grazing animal, living in small herds on the savanna. Lions sometimes kill rhinoceros calves, but the animals have no other enemies apart from humans.

The rhinoceros has small eyes and cannot see very far, but it makes up for this with very good hearing together with a superb sense of smell.

Rhinoceros babies start to grow their horns after about five weeks. They stay with their mothers for about five years.

THE BLACK RHINOCEROS

The black rhinoceros is actually grey, just like the white rhinoceros, but it is not quite as big. Its pointed snout is quite different from the wide snout of the white rhino. Instead of grazing on grass, it browses on bushes and uses its hooked lip to gather in branches. It usually lives alone and is rather bad-tempered.

The white rhino's wide snout is ideal for grazing. The name white rhino came from a bad translation of the African word *weid*, meaning wide.

The horn is very hard, but it is actually made of a mass of coarse hairs cemented together. The front horn can be well over 50 cm long.

SURVIVAL WATCH

Huge numbers of rhinos are killed for their horns, which many people think have magic powers. The white rhino was almost extinct some years ago, but about 4000 of them are now safely protected in nature reserves. The black rhino is still in great danger. In 1970 there were about 65,000 of these great beasts in Africa, but fewer than 3000 now remain. A Rhino Rescue Fund has been set up to save them.

Egrets often follow rhinos to feed on the insects stirred up by their huge feet. They sometimes perch on the rhinos' backs.

Rhinos love to wallow in muddy pools. This helps them to keep cool and also helps to get rid of ticks and other blood-sucking creatures.

Baboons – monkeys in the grass

These chacma baboons look rather like dogs, but they are actually big ground-living monkeys. They live in troops of about 40 individuals, ruled by one or two adult males. They sometimes kill small antelope, but usually eat smaller animals, including scorpions. Baboons also like fruit and vegetables, and often damage crops.

Baboons spend a lot of time grooming each other. This helps to keep all the members of the troop friendly with each other.

BABOON FACTS

● Chacma baboons are about 60 cm tall. They live in southern Africa.

● Baboons sometimes throw stones at their enemies.

The adult male has a large mane, which makes him look even bigger and fiercer when he faces a rival male or an enemy.

Adult baboons make a great fuss of their babies – as long as they behave. They smack them if they are being naughty.

The stripy zebra

Zebras are really just horses with stripes. They live in many parts of Africa, usually in small bands. Most bands consist of a stallion, or male, and a few mares and their foals. Some bands consist only of males. The bands often join up in the rainy season and then thousands of zebras can be seen feeding together on the fresh grass.

Zebras often mingle with other animals such as the wildebeest that you can see here, especially when they gather at the waterholes. There are always some animals ready to give the alarm if enemies appear.

No two zebras look exactly alike. The stripes may help them to recognize each other. They also help with camouflage.

Zebras are usually peaceful animals, but when necessary they defend themselves by kicking viciously with their hooves.

 ZEBRA FACTS

• Grevy's zebra, shown here, is the biggest zebra. It is about 150 cm high at the shoulder and has no belly stripes. It lives just north of the Equator in East Africa.

Grevy's zebra

• There are three kinds of zebras. Burchell's zebra, which you can see in the picture above, is the most common. The mountain zebra is similar, but has no stripes on its belly. It is found in south-west Africa.

The wandering wildebeest

The wildebeest is a large antelope living in huge herds on the African plains. The herds are nearly always on the move, searching for tender young grass. Babies are born at the beginning of the wet season, when there is plenty of new grass for them to eat. Lions follow the herds and eat some of the babies, but there are so many babies that most of them escape. The lions can't eat them all.

Some wildebeest herds contain over 10,000 animals. They create huge clouds of dust as they move over the dry plains. When they are frightened they can gallop along at speeds of more than 50 km/h.

WILDEBEEST FACTS

● Wildebeest means 'wild cow'. The animal is also called the gnu.

● Wildebeest are about 145 cm high at the shoulder and they weigh up to 270 kg.

DO YOU KNOW

Wildebeest herds drop tonnes of dung, but it is soon cleared up by swarms of dung beetles. The beetles often roll the dung into balls and bury it before eating it or laying eggs in it.

The wildebeest has a face rather like a cow, but it has a mane and a beard. Its curved horns measure up to 1 metre across.

Graceful Grant's gazelle

Grant's gazelle lives on the plains of East Africa. It eats grass and also browses on the scattered bushes. It can live without drinking so, unlike other antelope, it does not need to move around to find water.

 DO YOU KNOW

Baby gazelles hide in long grass. Their mothers chase away any jackals that get too near. If hyenas appear, the mother gazelles lead the babies to safety.

Grant's gazelle is about 85 cm high at the shoulder. If frightened, it flashes warnings to other gazelles with the white patch on its rump.

The springbuck – a great high-jumper

The springbuck is less than 1 metre high, but it can leap more than 3 metres into the air from a standing start. This little antelope grazes in small herds on the dry plains of South Africa.

When the springbuck is alarmed it leaps high into the air and raises the crest of white hairs on its back. This warns other animals to look out for danger.

 DO YOU KNOW

The springbuck is the national emblem of South Africa. The country used to be home to millions of springbuck, but most of them were killed by hunters.

The lion – king of the savanna

The lion is the largest meat-eater on the African plains. It lives in groups of up to 30 animals and feeds mainly on zebras and wildebeest. Most groups contain just one adult male, with several females and their cubs. Larger groups may have two or three adult males. The females do most of the hunting. They work together to chase and catch the prey and the meat is then shared between all the members of the group.

Lions are really quite lazy animals. They eat large meals and spend the rest of their time sleeping or just lying in the shade. They do not eat every day.

The male's bushy mane makes him look even bigger and stronger than he is. It helps him to scare off rival males.

 DO YOU KNOW

Lions once lived all over Africa and southern Asia. They are still common in parts of Africa, but only about 300 lions remain in Asia. They all live in a reserve in north-west India. They have smaller manes than African lions and bushier tails.

Asiatic lion

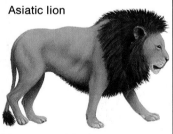

The male's roar can be heard several kilometres away. The female does not have such a loud roar. Cubs cannot roar at all.

Young lion cubs are spotted. Cubs are lively, and spend a lot of their time playing with each other and also with their mothers.

LION FACTS

- A group of lions is known as a pride.

- A male lion is about 1 metre high at the shoulder and can weigh up to 250 kg.

- Lions have large appetites and can eat 35 kg of meat in a single meal.

The female, called a lioness, is smaller than the male and has no mane. A group's lionesses are very often all sisters.

Busy weaver birds

Weaver birds live all over the grasslands and forests of Africa. They make wonderful nests by weaving grass and strips of palm leaves together. The nests often look like hanging baskets. There are many different kinds of weaver birds and each one has its own nest pattern.

Village weavers often nest in palm trees in or near villages. Their nests weigh the branches down like huge fruits.

The male builds the nest, using his beak to weave the strips in and out. He always starts off by making a ring.

If the male does not manage to attract a mate in a few days, he pulls the nest to pieces and starts all over again.

THE WORLD'S BIGGEST NESTS

Sociable weavers make the world's biggest nests. Many birds work together to make a thatched roof over part of a tree. Each pair then nests in the thatch. Some nests house over 100 pairs of birds.

The nest can be 5 metres across

The secretary bird

The secretary bird is a long-legged cousin of the hawks and eagles. It lives on the tree-dotted savanna of Africa and spends most of its time on the ground. Farmers like it because it kills snakes and rats. It also eats small tortoises, but its main foods are locusts and lizards. Secretary birds build big nests in thorn trees.

? DO YOU KNOW

Secretary birds like fires. They catch lots of small animals driven out by the flames sweeping over the grass.

These long feathers look like the quill pens that office workers once used – and that's how the bird got its name.

The secretary bird has an unusual way of killing its prey – it uses its long legs and sturdy feet to trample its victims to death.

Secretary birds live in areas with fairly short grass. This makes it easy for them to see their prey as they walk along.

SECRETARY FACTS

● The secretary bird is over 1 metre tall and has a wingspan of about 2 metres. It can fly well, but needs a long take-off run.

● Chicks stay in the nest for a long time – about 200 days.

The honey-loving ratel

The ratel is a fierce, badger-like animal from Africa and India. It eats all sorts of other animals, but its favourite food is honey. It works in partnership with a little bird called a honey-guide. The bird is very good at finding bees' nests, but it needs the ratel to open them. The ratel gets its honey and the bird gets the bees' grubs and some of the honeycomb.

Honey-guides often lead people to wild bees' nests. The people take the honey, but always leave some honeycomb for the birds.

The bees usually nest in hollow trees or among rocks. The nest consists of wax honey-combs full of honey and bee grubs.

When a honey-guide finds a nest it calls loudly to attract a ratel. The ratel follows the bird to the nest.

The ratel's thick black and white fur gives it plenty of protection against stings from the angry bees as it breaks open the nest.

RATEL FACTS

• The ratel is often called a honey badger. It is 70 cm long and weighs up to 12 kg.

• The ratel gives off an awful smell, which almost puts the bees to sleep so that they find it hard to sting.

A ratel's strong claws can easily push rocks away or rip open tree trunks to reach the bees' nests.

The spotted hyaena

Packs of hyaenas roam the African plains, looking for any kind of meat to eat. They often kill wildebeest and zebras. At other times they drive other animals, including lions, from their kills and steal the food.

HYAENA FACTS

● The spotted hyaena is the largest of three types of hyaenas found in Africa.

● It is sometimes called the laughing hyaena because of its cackling calls.

Hyaenas waste very little food. With their great teeth they can even crush the bones of their prey.

Vultures – nature's refuse collectors

Vultures are ugly birds, but they do a good job. They eat up dead animals on the plains of Africa. Vultures have bare heads and necks because feathers would get very dirty from the messy bodies they feed from.

Vultures queue up to feed. There may be several kinds in the queue. The biggest ones feed first and the smallest ones have to make do with the scraps that the big ones leave behind.

The bison – America's biggest animal

The bison is a huge wild cousin of our farm cattle. It is often called a buffalo, but the real buffalo is an African mammal. Bison live in small family groups consisting of a bull and a cow and their youngsters, but these groups often join up to form larger herds. They travel hundreds of kilometres each year as they search out the best feeding areas for each season.

The bison has massive shoulders, which are made to look even bigger by the thick hair on the front part of its body.

SURVIVAL WATCH

Millions of bison once roamed the North American prairies, providing food for the Indians. But European settlers killed nearly all the bison. By 1889 there were only about 500 left. Luckily, these were protected in nature reserves and there are now several thousand of them.

BISON FACTS

• Bison weigh up to 1000 kg and are nearly 2 metres high at the shoulder.

• The European bison, also called the wisent, became extinct in the wild in 1919. Small herds still survive in forest parks in Eastern Europe.

The pronghorn

The pronghorn is America's fastest land animal. It can run at speeds of over 70 km/h, covering 8 metres with each bound. Each male defends a territory from March until October. The strongest males get the best feeding areas. They mate with any females visiting their territories in the autumn.

PRONGHORN FACTS

● Pronghorns are about 85 cm high at the shoulder. They grow a new set of horns every year.

● They will eat all kinds of plants, from grasses and shrubs to prickly cacti.

Large eyes give the pronghorn excellent all-round vision. Long eye-lashes shade their eyes from the sun.

The white rump acts as a signal to other pronghorns when danger appears.

SURVIVAL WATCH

Like the bison, the pronghorn was extremely common until the 19th Century. European settlers then killed most of them and they almost died out. Their numbers have now grown again, but some areas where prong-horns live are being threatened by the oil and coal industries.

Large shock-absorbing hooves take the strain when the pronghorn's feet crash down on the ground.

The prairie marmot

Prairie marmots are burrowing squirrels which live on the North American prairies. They live in groups called coteries. Each group has its own system of tunnels a metre or more below the surface, and each system has several entrances. Marmots feed on grass and other low-growing plants. They regularly visit marmots in neighbouring coteries in the summer and sometimes move in with them.

 MARMOT FACTS

● The prairie marmot is often called a prairie dog because of its bark.

● The prairie marmot is about 30 cm long.

Marmots greet other members of the same coterie by giving them a kiss.

If a marmot spots a hawk or a coyote, it barks loudly and wags its tail to warn its neighbours of the danger.

Each burrow entrance is surrounded by a mound of soil, which serves as a look-out post and also prevents flooding.

DO YOU KNOW

Neighbouring coteries link up to form towns. Some towns cover over 50 hectares, but in the days before settlers started ploughing up the prairies the towns were even bigger. Some were over 100 km across and contained millions of animals.

The singing coyote

Coyotes are small North American cousins of the wolf. They are often called prairie wolves, although they also live in the forests and mountains. They eat all sorts of small animals and usually hunt alone or in pairs. They also eat dead creatures and often feed on other animals' left-overs. Coyotes occasionally kill sheep, but they do not do a lot of damage. They are protected by law in the United States and Canada.

DO YOU KNOW

Coyotes are intelligent animals and many have learned that there is plenty of food in and around towns. They come into the towns at night to raid the rubbish bins.

Coyotes often breed with domestic dogs to produce coy-dogs.

Coyotes produce their howling barks at dusk and dawn. All the surrounding coyotes join in the chorus.

Coyotes sometimes join up to form small packs which can catch deer and other large animals.

COYOTE FACTS

● The coyote is up to about 100 cm long, and its bushy tail is 30–40 cm long.

● Coyotes keep the same mate all their lives. The female may have over 15 pups in one litter, although ten is more usual.

The saiga of the steppes

The saiga is a strange-looking antelope from the cold grasslands of Asia. People used to hunt it for the sake of its horns, which were thought to have magical healing properties. Only a few hundred animals were left by 1930, but the USSR government banned hunting for a time and several million saiga now roam the steppes again.

SAIGA FACTS

● The saiga is about 80 cm high and weighs up to 50 kg.

● Females usually have twins, which is unusual among hoofed mammals.

● The saiga's coat turns white in the winter.

Only the male saiga has horns. These are about 30 cm long and almost transparent.

PRZEWALSKI'S HORSE

This is the largest animal of the cold grasslands of Central Asia. The horse is probably extinct in the wild, but a few hundred animals survive in zoos and wildlife parks. Przewalski's horse is thought to be the ancestor of all domestic horses.

The swollen snout contains a maze of passages which warm and moisten the air before it gets into the saiga's lungs.

The hare

Hares of various kinds graze on nearly all the world's grasslands. This one is the brown hare from Europe and Asia. Hares do not live in burrows like rabbits. Their babies are born in the grass with all their fur and with their eyes open.

You can tell the brown hare from a rabbit by its long black-tipped ears and longer legs.

DO YOU KNOW

In the spring, hares chase about and leap high into the air. The males even have 'boxing matches' and get so excited that we call them mad March hares.

The common hamster

Hamsters are burrowing animals. The common hamster is up to 28 cm long and lives on the grassy steppes of the USSR and eastern Europe. It is also found in grain fields. It feeds at night, mainly on seeds.

Hamsters collect their food in large cheek pouches. They then store it in their burrows until they want it.

DO YOU KNOW

The attractive 12 cm long golden hamster has become one of the world's most popular pets. All golden hamsters are descended from a single litter of 12 babies found in Syria in 1930. They now come in many different colours and there are both long-haired and short-haired types.

The nosy anteater

This weird animal which roams the plains of South America is a giant anteater. It opens ant nests with its huge claws, and then mops up the insects with its long sticky tongue. It can flick its tongue out about three times a second to pick up the ants.

Giant anteaters are about 2 metres long. Mothers carry their babies around on their backs for up to a year.

The anteater finds ant nests with its keen sense of smell. The animal has no teeth.

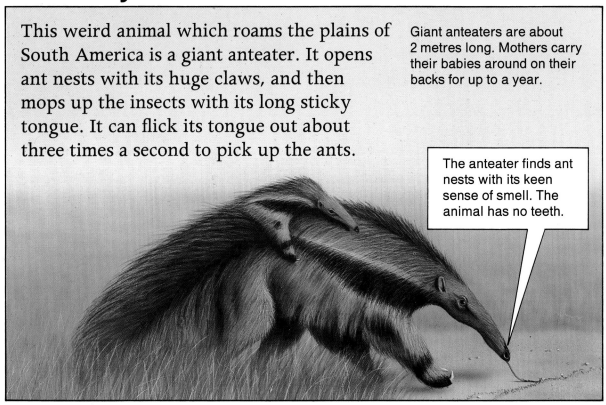

The armoured armadillo

This nine-banded armadillo eats all sorts of animals and plants, but is particularly fond of ants and termites. It can eat 40,000 of them in a single meal. Although its armour is heavy, the animal can swim well. It swallows air and this helps it to float.

? DO YOU KNOW

Armadillos live only in America. The nine-banded armadillo is the commonest type.

Armadillo armour is made of bony plates. Some species can protect themselves by rolling into balls.

The rhea

The rhea lives on the plains of South America and is America's largest bird. It can't fly, but it is a fast and agile runner. It spreads its wings like sails when changing direction at speed. Rheas eat all sorts of plant and animal food, especially insects and lizards. The male rhea mates with as many females as he can and looks after all the eggs and chicks.

 RHEA FACTS

● Rheas weigh up to 20 kg and can run at about 60 km/h.

● Rheas are rarer than they used to be because more wild grassland areas are now used for farming.

 DO YOU KNOW

Rheas, emus, and ostriches look very much alike, but they are not closely related. They live in three separate continents and they look alike only because they are all built for life on the grasslands. The rhea is the smallest of the three.

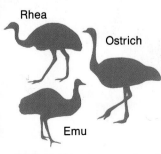

Rhea

Ostrich

Emu

The male rhea makes a simple nest on the ground and may look after more than 50 eggs and chicks.

31

The guinea pig

Guinea pigs are not pigs. They are rodents, which means they are related to rats and mice. They originally came from South America, and their wild relatives still graze on the grasslands there. These wild ones are called cavies.

GUINEA PIG FACTS

● South American Indians rear guinea pigs for food.

● Guinea pigs make super pets and there are dozens of varieties, in a range of colours.

A pet guinea pig

Bouncing maras

Maras are long-legged cousins of the guinea pig. They graze the grasslands of Argentina and are often called Patagonian cavies. Male and female maras pair for life, but they live in groups in the breeding season and guard their babies in shared dens.

Male maras spend a lot of their time sitting up and watching for signs of danger.

Maras look rather like miniature deer as they bound along on their long legs.

Budgerigars in the wild

Budgerigars, or budgies, are small parrots which swarm in huge flocks over the Australian grasslands. They feed mainly on grass seeds, although they also upset farmers by eating a lot of wheat. During the breeding season they nest in tree holes, but at other times the flocks are always on the move. Once they have eaten all the seeds in one area, they fly to new feeding grounds.

? DO YOU KNOW

The budgie is the most popular pet bird. It was brought to Europe in 1840. Since then, blue, yellow, grey and white budgies have been bred from the original birds.

Wild budgerigars are all bright green with yellow heads and blue tails. They are about 17 cm long.

The red kangaroo

The red kangaroo is the largest of Australia's native mammals. It is as tall as a person and weighs up to 90 kg. But its baby is not much bigger than a cherry when it is born. The baby has to spend several months feeding on milk in its mother's pouch. Red kangaroos live all over the open grasslands. They walk on all four feet when grazing, but at other times they bound along on their big back legs. Males often fight by kicking opponents with their back feet.

SURVIVAL WATCH

Red and great grey kangaroos are very plentiful. However, many of the smaller kangaroos are in real danger from the dogs and foxes that were brought to Australia by humans.

The baby kangaroo is called a joey. It lives in its mother's pouch for about eight months before making its first journey outside.

Kangaroos rest on their big hind feet and use their thick tail as an extra support. Sharp claws cause nasty wounds when kangaroos fight.

A kangaroo's face is quite like that of a deer or an antelope. This is because all these animals have teeth and jaws designed for grazing.

Kangaroos live in herds called mobs. Each mob usually has up to 12 members. They have no real home and wander all over the place.

There are about 55 kinds of kangaroo-like animals in Australia and New Guinea. The great grey kangaroo is very similar to the red kangaroo, but the others are all much smaller. Many are called wallabies and potoroos. Like most of Australia's native mammals, they are all marsupials, which means that they carry their babies in pouches.

Wombats (below) are burrowing marsupials of southern Australia. They look like small bears, but they are gentle grazing animals and they often make delightful pets.

The male kangaroo can be 2 metres tall. He is called a boomer, and is much redder than the female. She is much smaller, and is called a flier.

Tireless termites

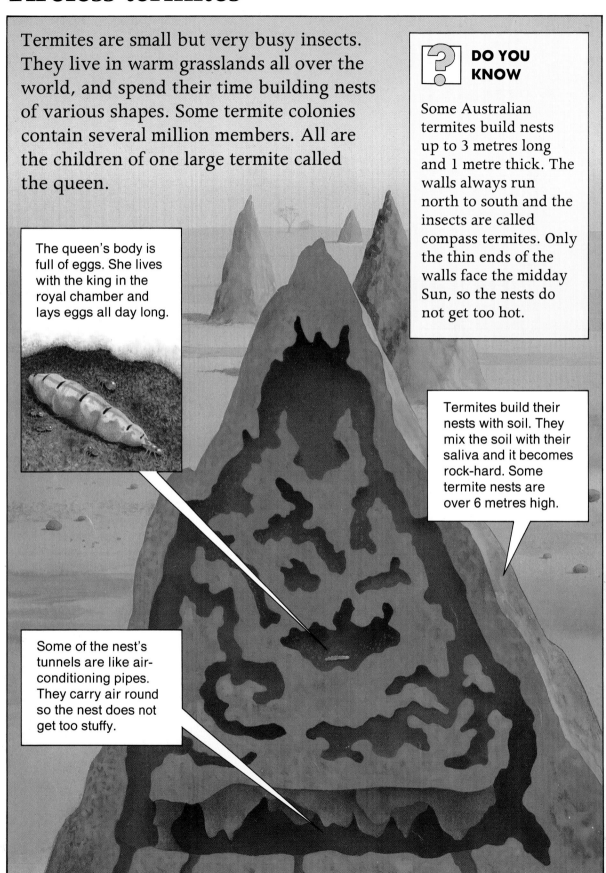

Termites are small but very busy insects. They live in warm grasslands all over the world, and spend their time building nests of various shapes. Some termite colonies contain several million members. All are the children of one large termite called the queen.

DO YOU KNOW

Some Australian termites build nests up to 3 metres long and 1 metre thick. The walls always run north to south and the insects are called compass termites. Only the thin ends of the walls face the midday Sun, so the nests do not get too hot.

The queen's body is full of eggs. She lives with the king in the royal chamber and lays eggs all day long.

Termites build their nests with soil. They mix the soil with their saliva and it becomes rock-hard. Some termite nests are over 6 metres high.

Some of the nest's tunnels are like air-conditioning pipes. They carry air round so the nest does not get too stuffy.

The emu

The emu is Australia's biggest bird. It can run at speeds of up to 50 km/h. It can also swim, but it is much too heavy to fly. Emus live mainly on the grasslands and roam around in small flocks. They eat almost anything, but plants and insects are their main foods. Emus travel long distances in search of food and water and often raid farm crops in the dry season. Emus are nosy birds and not at all afraid of people.

Emus are covered with fluffy feathers that completely hide their tiny wings.

DO YOU KNOW

The male emu builds the nest and sits on the eggs for about eight weeks. Since he rarely leaves the nest during this time, he gets little to eat or drink for a long time.

EMU FACTS

● Male emus growl and grunt, but the call of the female is very different – more like the beating of a drum.

● The emu can grow to about 1.8 metres tall – about as high as people. The only bigger bird is the ostrich, at 2.5 metres.

Grasslands in danger

The world's grasslands are shrinking rapidly. Farming is a big threat to them because the grasslands are ideal for ploughing up and growing crops. Changes in the climate also threaten the grasslands, especially in Africa. Vast areas of the savanna along the southern edge of the Sahara are becoming drier and steadily turning into desert. Many of the grassland animals are dying out because their habitats are being destroyed.

Illegal hunting is another problem faced by many grassland animals such as rhinos, even when they live in special reserves. These reserves are so big, the wardens cannot stamp out hunting altogether.

 GUNS ARE TO BLAME

People lived on the world's grasslands for thousands of years without greatly reducing the numbers of animals that lived there. The trouble really began when people started killing grassland animals with guns. Millions of bison were reduced to just a few hundred within a few years of people bringing guns to North America. The same thing happened to many of Africa's grassland animals too.

Useful words

Browse   To nibble the shoots and leaves of trees, shrubs and other tall plants. Because of their long necks, giraffes can browse on higher branches than other animals.

Camouflage   The way in which animals avoid the attention of their enemies by resembling their surroundings or blending in with them. The animals are then not easy to see.

Climate   The general weather conditions of an area, due largely to its position on the Earth's surface.

Colony   A group of animals living closely together and helping each other. Each member of the colony usually has a particular job.

Domestic   Kept and looked after by people and not living in the wild. Dogs and horses are examples of animals that have been domesticated.

Extinct   No longer existing anywhere in the world. Many types of animals are close to extinction, and if they are allowed to die out they will never be seen again.

Grazing   Feeding on grasses and other low-growing plants, and usually nibbling them down to ground level.

Grooming   The action of cleaning and combing the fur – especially the fur of another animal living in the same group.

Herd   The name given to any large group of hoofed mammals, such as zebra or antelope, which live and feed together.

Mammal   Any member of the large group of animals that feed their babies with milk from the mother's body. Mammals are warm-blooded and are usually covered with hair or fur.

Marsupial   Any member of the group of mammals in which the babies are carried about in a pouch on the mother's body. Most marsupials live in Australia.

Native   Living naturally in a certain area and not introduced from somewhere else. Kangaroos are native to Australia, while foxes were brought to that country by humans.

Nature reserve   An area set aside to protect wild plants and animals – often rare ones which are in danger of dying out.

Prey   Any animal that is caught and eaten by another animal. The hunting animal is called a predator.

Rodent   Any member of the mouse and guinea pig group of animals, with chisel-like front teeth which are used to chew or gnaw through food and other materials. These teeth keep on growing throughout the animals' lives to make up for the constant wearing away at the tip.

Savanna   The name given to the African grasslands, especially those in the tropical areas.

Tropical   Concerning the warmer parts of the world, close to the Equator.

Waterhole   A pond where animals regularly gather to drink.

Index